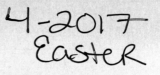

4-2017
Easter

To:

My first Born Grandson Liam
Anthony Baca

From:

Grandma Kam :)
You are always precious in my
heart sweetheart

Good Good Father

Chris Tomlin
and Pat Barrett
Illustrated by Lorna Hussey

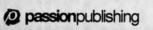 passion publishing

 Tommy NELSON

A Division of Thomas Nelson Publishers

Good Good Father

© 2016 by Chris Tomlin and Pat Barrett

Published in Nashville, Tennessee, by Tommy Nelson. Tommy Nelson is an imprint of Thomas Nelson. Thomas Nelson is a registered trademark of HarperCollins Christian Publishing, Inc.

Published in partnership with Passion Publishing

Illustrated by Lorna Hussey

Tommy Nelson titles may be purchased in bulk for educational, business, fund-raising, or sales promotional use. For information, please e-mail SpecialMarkets@ThomasNelson.com.

ISBN-13: 978-0-7180-8695-4

Library of Congress Cataloging-in-Publication Data is on file.

Printed in the USA

16 17 18 19 20 PC 10 9 8 7 6 5

LETTER TO READERS

From the moment I (Chris) heard the opening verse of the song "Good Good Father" written by Pat Barrett and Tony Brown, the lyrics hit me in such a special way. We all have a picture of what we think God is like, and that view shapes our faith.

As dads, Pat and I want our kids to understand that God isn't some distant God. In fact, God is often described as a Father. What an amazing concept for boys and girls to grasp from a young age! It's out of this heart that Pat and I wrote the story of Tucker, a little bear in need of help from the good King who lives in the castle where the door is always open.

As you read *Good Good Father* with the children in your life, we hope it touches your heart. But more than that, we hope you experience the goodness of our good, good Father and His love for you and your little ones.

Chris Tomlin
Pat Barrett

A colorful kite soared in the sky, and then *whoosh!*—it caught on an oak tree branch.

"Don't worry. I can help!" Tucker called, tugging the kite this way and that.

Tucker was a little bear. Helping others made him happy . . . and his friends needed lots of help.

Some bears were **always fighting** . . .

some bears were **sick** . . .

some bears **couldn't read** . . .

some bears were **hungry** . . .

and some bears were **sad**.

Tucker didn't
know how to
help his friends.

"I could ask the King for help!" Tucker cried. "Maybe, just maybe, if I give him the perfect gift, he will help us."

So off Tucker went on a journey to see the good King who lived in the castle where the door was always open.

It wasn't long before a group of big, strong raccoons blocked Tucker's path.

"Stop!" one raccoon ordered. "What do you want?"

"I w-w-want to take the King the perfect gift, but-but-but I don't know what to choose," Tucker explained.

"The King is a good warrior," the raccoon said. "Why don't you give him this shield?"

"The King will keep you safe!" cheered the other raccoons.

Down the road, an owl swooped down in front of Tucker.

"*Hoot, hoot!*" the owl called out. "What would you like to learn?"

"I'm trying to figure out the perfect gift to take to the King," Tucker replied.

"The King teaches from his wise book," the owl told him. "I'm certain the King would be pleased if you gave him something to read."

As Tucker walked away, the owl hooted, "Go see the King. He is a good teacher!"

As he walked, Tucker spotted foxes wearing long white jackets.

"How are you feeling?" asked a concerned fox.

"I feel fine, but some of the bears in my town are sick," Tucker replied. "I'm on my way to see the King and ask for his help."

"Here, take these bandages as a gift," the fox said. "The King is a good doctor."

More confused than ever, Tucker sat to rest.

"Are you here for a snack?" a squirrel asked.

"Actually, I'm trying to find the perfect gift for the King," Tucker explained, looking around. "Wow! You have so many yummy-looking fruits and vegetables!"

"Why don't you take
the King these seeds?"
the squirrel suggested.
"The King is a good farmer.
He will help you grow food."

Far away Tucker heard music . . . and singing . . . and
laughter. He followed the sounds until he
spotted some happy turtles.

"Jump on in—now's your chance! This turtle town just loves to dance!" a turtle sang. "We used to be sad. But now, everything is a celebration because of the King!"

"What kind of gift do you think he would like?" Tucker asked.

"Give the King this violin," the turtle said. "He's a good musician. The King will bring you joy!"

All the animals Tucker met had told him different stories about the King and what the perfect gift would be. But Tucker still didn't know what to give him.

He looked up to the castle at the top of the tall hill. As it always was, the door was wide open.

Tucker tiptoed toward the open door.

"Tucker!" The King ran toward him with a huge smile. "I'm so glad you're here! It looks like you need my help."

"My friends are in trouble, and I thought if I brought you the perfect gift, you would help us," Tucker explained shyly.

"You brought the *perfect* gift!" the King said with great love. "Now, let's go help your friends."

Tucker wasn't sure
which gift was the perfect
one. Even so, he hurried
off with the King.

On their journey back to the little bear's town, Tucker asked question after question.

"Are you a warrior?"
"Yes," the King answered.

"Are you a teacher?"
"Yes," the King repeated.

"Are you a doctor?"

"Are you a farmer?"

"Are you a musician?"

"Yes, yes, and yes," the King patiently replied.

"But how can you be all of these things?" the little bear asked.

The King smiled. "I am all of these things because I am a Good Father."

Tucker didn't understand.

Soon the King and the little bear reached Tucker's town. When the bears saw the King, one by one they bowed down. The King walked through the town and gave help to everyone who needed it.

Most of all, the King, the Good Father, loved them.

Tucker said to the King, "Now I see! You are not only a Good Father—you are a Good *Good* Father.

A Good Good Father protects us.

A Good Good Father teaches us.

A Good Good Father makes us well.

A Good Good Father gives us what we need.

A Good Good Father fills life with music and laughter.

And most of all, a Good Good Father loves us . . .

"Dear King, I have one more question. Which gift was the perfect gift?" Tucker asked.

"*You are the perfect gift!*" the King told the little bear. "You came to me when you needed help. You trusted me. You bring me great joy, and I love you with all my heart, the same way I love all my children."

Tucker, curled up with sleepy eyes and a full heart, whispered, "You really are a Good Good Father."